HOUSES OF OLD TORONTO

HOUSES OF OLD TORONTO

Paintings by William Roberts
Text by Mary Anne Roberts

Pagurian Press Limited
Toronto

ISBN 0-88932-063-2
Printed and bound in Canada

For
Mary
Richard
Corinne
Elizabeth
Gwyneth
Jesse

Contents

Introduction

Long before I ever saw Toronto, I had heard the family stories about the old days when my mother and grandparents had lived there. My Great-Grandparents Levasseur had come up to Toronto from Little Rock, Arkansas, after the American Civil War and there my grandmother met and married my grandfather, William Bissett.

Grandfather ran a store on Yonge Street not far from Eaton's but competition from Timothy was so fierce, he had to give it up and go "on the road," selling china and toys for Cassidy's, an importing firm. Family tradition had it that Timothy Eaton offered Grandfather a job running his china department and he could have had the job whenever he wanted.

My grandparents lived in the area around Spadina below Dundas Street. Here my mother was born and attended the old Catholic school at Dundas and McCaul Streets. She told many stories of Toronto and of her friend Gladys Smith, better known as Mary Pickford. The family spent summer holidays on Toronto Island and my mother had her own small sailboat.

After the turn of the century, the family joined the migration west and moved to Calgary. And so it was that I came to be born in British Columbia.

I didn't see Toronto until 1941. I was stationed at the Number One Manning Depot at the Canadian National Exhibition grounds during induction into the Air Force. We marched a lot around the Exhibition grounds and occasionally up lower Spadina. I remember the Casino Stage Theatre, the Queen Street pawn shops, and the gypsies along Queen Street behind their heavily curtained windows.

After the war, I returned to Toronto to attend the Ontario College of Art. I took an etching class from Nick Hornyansky who had a great enthusiasm for old buildings. I think the first thing I did was a soft ground etching of the old firehall, still standing west of Spadina on College Street. During the next five or six years I made many drawings all over the downtown area of the city. The first real encouragement came from a watercolour I did of a wonderful restaurant on York Street, just south of Queen Street, called Bank's Lunch.

At the time I was working at Brigden's, Artists, Printers and Engravers, located at Richmond and University. That area was rich in early architectural marvels—row houses, mansions, factories, cottages. I did many watercolours and drawings of these buildings after work and on weekends, but nothing much came of these efforts. Then in 1950 or 1951 I submitted two paintings, a watercolour entitled ''Bank's Lunch'' and an egg tempera, to the annual exhibition of the Ontario Society of Artists held at the Art Gallery of Ontario. Both were accepted by the Society and the watercolour, ''Bank's Lunch,'' was purchased on opening night for thirty-five dollars. This was my first professional sale, and an encouraging event, as sales were rare at those exhibitions.

I continued painting downtown, mainly in watercolour, casein, and egg tempera. Then in 1952 I went to Europe on a painting trip and painted towns, lighthouses, and buildings mostly in England and Spain. When I returned to Toronto and work in commercial art, I continued my practice of painting the city, but the experience of the English countryside had encouraged me to experiment in painting pure landscape, without buildings, and I began to make weekend trips around southern Ontario.

At about that time I met the late John Martin, an immensely civilized man who was keenly interested in architecture and history. He had produced two unique, illustrated booklets about the architecture of Waterloo and Huron Counties, and showed me many unusual aspects of Toronto and Ontario architecture and history.

When choosing a suitable building for a painting subject, I was mainly interested in what was visually pleasing. I really wasn't looking for examples of fine architecture because at that time I didn't know that much about the subject. What appealed was simplicity of design and the sort of character an old building gets from its wrinkles. As far as painting is concerned, I have never minded modern store fronts. Generally, modernization of old stores extended only as high as a step-ladder could reach, so that the result was a pleasing contrast between a jazzy ''light lunch'' sign and a well-proportioned building with a subtle patina above it.

In painting the pictures for this book, I realize I have used these same criteria in choosing the subjects. The buildings I enjoyed doing most were the Modern Furniture Store, the last painting in the book, and the three stores on Yonge Street. These stores, Number 42, Number 44, and Number 46, in their present condition of "pleasing decay," are a visual feast. The contrast of the shiny black tile and the worn brick, the rust stains, the store signs—all are part of their attraction. The Modern Furniture Store does not have the textural variations of the Yonge Street stores but offers instead rich colours and beautiful simplicity of form—the sparkle of chrome and the reflected light against the dark windows, framed by bright red and blue.

In these, as in some of the other pictures, I have used the reflections in the windows as paintings within paintings; the reflections in the glass themselves form abstract paintings.

All the buildings are located in that section of Toronto bounded by Dundas, Yonge, and Parliament Streets. (The one exception, Campbell House, was moved from its original location here.) This area has a great number of interesting buildings since it is the oldest part of the city and has changed as the city grew. I have been familiar with the neighbourhood for many years and this seems to have provided me with a central focus for the book.

Besides this geographical boundary, there are also the restrictions in size and format imposed by the requirements of publishing. Within *these* limitations, I have tried to choose a variety of buildings according to architectural style, date, and purpose. They range over a large part of the nineteenth century, from 1822 to 1894. The styles are Georgian to late Victorian; they are humble and grand, public and private. The variety of their use is intended to show a sense of the community.

I included Massey Hall for reasons of community — it has important social and historical connections with the city. But it presented the most problems. I had to take two runs at it. The building has such a hodge-podge of detail, windows cut in and windows filled in, and jumble of fire escapes. Its one redeeming feature, as far as the painting of it goes, is the red doors.

The first painting I did was the small corner store at King and Berkeley. One of its attractions is the Pepsi sign out front, a bright contrast to the broken plaster and drab appearance of the rest of the building. I find it more pleasing visually than the slicked-up Campbell House.

Mackenzie House has good classic proportions, subtle colour and texture of brick, and a pleasing, worn look.

The row houses of a later period on Mutual Street are more humble than Mackenzie House. Their attraction lies in their individual treatments. Although they are small and identical, their owners have asserted their individuality in bright, careful paint jobs.

In painting St. Lawrence Hall, I could have chosen any side. The expected view is usually the King Street entrance, but the simpler west elevation serves to give greater importance to the clock and bell tower.

The seventh Post Office, now the Argus Corporation offices on Toronto Street, appeals as a good exercise in the proportions of the golden section, and as an example of classic simplicity.

De La Salle and Dominion Brewery are similar both in style and degree of decay. De La Salle was chosen because it had been a schoolhouse, but it is personally satisfying for its boarded-up windows and its monochromatic blandness. The Dominion Brewery is stronger texturally because of its peeling paint and rust stains.

Low key colour tone is a quality of the National Hotel as well. Of the old hotels in the area, the National was picked for its colour and window reflections.

All Saints' Church suits my painting manner. The big downtown cathedrals are somewhat overwhelming. I like All Saints' for its patterned brickwork; it has a simple, country look about it and I like its present uses.

There are two firehalls in the neighbourhood — the Firehall Theatre on Berkeley Street and the Old Firehall on Lombard. I chose the Lombard Street hall because it faces south, giving good shadows morning and afternoon. At first I didn't like the golden canopy or the cute little trees but I found they worked well with the red doors and the Banff-Springs-Hotel-style of stonework.

The Gooderham flat-iron building is a striking landmark due to its central location and distinctive shape. It was a good subject for the narrow vertical highlight on its prow beside the dark shadowy side, the copper roof, the razzle-dazzle fire escape, and even the contrast of the stop-light and the dark background.

The offices of Consumers' Gas Company, Toronto's oldest public utility, are pleasing for their quiet decoration and their wonderfully reflective windows, so abstract against the formal lines of the building. The gas works are appealing for their warm colour and muted windows and are also a good example of late Victorian industrial architecture.

It seemed appropriate to include a bank in the book, and I at first preferred the nearby Bank of Commerce which is more restrained than the Bank of Montreal. However, I found that this flamboyant, overly decorated, marcelled, and plumed dowager of a bank provided a relief to the more formal styles of many of the other buildings.

In these paintings I have not held a mirror up to the buildings. They are not faithful renderings, as I have treated them fairly freely. They give an impression of lavish detail but a comparison with their life-sized subjects will show a good deal of simplification.

The buildings which I have chosen to paint, together with many others of their time and kind, have served us well. I hope they may continue to do so for many years. But as all things change, if they must be replaced, may it be done with structures as functional, beautiful, and well built as these. If they are to be restored, may it be done with intelligence, care, and love.

William Roberts

HOUSES OF OLD TORONTO

Corner Store

The shabby little building at the corner of King and Berkeley Streets was not always the restaurant or corner store that its appearance might suggest. Rather, it spent its early years as a saloon, sometimes euphemistically styled a hotel, but what temperance advocates were pleased to vilify as a "low grog shop" or a "tippling house."

When Toronto became a city, Berkeley Street was the eastern limit, and up until mid-century there were only scattered buildings in the area. It is possible the store was already standing here in 1856, but the first positive reference to it is in 1861 when it was owned by John Taylor and operated by John Matthews, at an annual rent of $140, under the name Garibaldi House.

Management of the saloon passed next to Hugh Taylor who was sixty-four in 1864; ownership was retained by John Taylor but shared jointly with Thomas and George Taylor. It was quite likely a family arrangement and Hugh was probably the father of the other three.

During the seventies Thomas Seaborn was the tavern keeper, although he did not own the place which he called the Somersetshire Hotel. Assessment rolls reveal the rather surprising fact that these premises, twenty-four feet by twenty-five feet, housed a

william Roberts CORNER STORE

family of eighteen plus three boarders. By 1878, however, Thomas Seaborn had been reduced to the status of "labourer" and William Irwin was running Irwin's Hotel. (John Irwin had been owner when Seaborn was tenant, so it appears to have been a case of inheritance.) Irwin kept the hotel through the eighties but temperance legislation aimed at reducing the liquor traffic forced the small saloon keeper out of business in the nineties. In 1894 Alexander Sleater sold cigars and tobacco here; by the middle of the decade it was simply a vacant store.

During the nineteenth century whiskey was cheap and plentiful, if not particularly palatable, and drinking it was often a two-fisted and violent affair. The magnitude of the problem is well illustrated by a very early temperance pledge in New Jersey in the 1820s, which involved the promise not to drink more than a pint of hard liquor a day.

Originally, wine, beer, and cider were regarded as relatively harmless; distilled spirits were sobriety's major enemy. According to Noah Webster's little speller of 1866:

> Rum, gin, brandy, and whiskey are destructive enemies to mankind.
> They destroy more lives than wars, famine, and pestilence.

But . . .

> Beer is an excellent drink for the table.

As time went on, the target of the temperance supporters included all intoxicating beverages and they sought, not simply a moderation of excessive drinking, but total abstinence.

Having a strong belief in the essential depravity of mankind, temperance advocates felt the only sure way to eradicate the evil was to eliminate all temptation. This dismal view of human nature was expressed in Lyman Cobb's Spelling Book of 1835, written especially for children:

> Were the life of man prolonged, he would become such a proficient
> in villainy, that it would be necessary to drown the world again, or to
> burn it.

In 1850 the official number of Toronto establishments licensed to sell liquor was listed as 152 taverns and 206 beer shops. The newspaper, *The Examiner*, on the contrary, referred to six or seven hundred liquor establishments operating in the city.

By 1874 the number of legal liquor sellers stood at 533 and, as ever, there were numerous bootleggers. Two years later the newly formed Women's Christian Temperance Union petitioned City Council to restrict the number of liquor licences. Council listened to the ladies and cut back the number of liquor licences to 215, shop licences to 100, and raised the licence fee to $200. These numbers were further reduced in 1886 to 200 taverns and 68 shops, and the regulations compelling hotel keepers to provide sufficient accommodation for the travelling public were more strictly enforced.

By 1890 the little corner store was squeezed out of the liquor trade. From 1900 until World War I it was a barber shop, owned first by William Spears and then by G. L. Arbuckle. During the war it was a butcher shop. In the twenties and thirties it became a grocery store with three successive proprietors, William Harding, Arthur Neale, and Mike Strawchen. Not only did the store provide the owners with a livelihood, but a home as well, with the residence entrance on Berkeley Street.

During the last years of the Depression the store was vacant but it was revived as the Central Lunch during World War II. It has remained a restaurant since — the Venice Lunch, Lab's Grill, and, most recently, the Hungarian Restaurant. Today it is vacant once again, and, unless someone rejuvenates it, all the history of the little building shall have been written.

Gooderham Building

The Gooderham Building occupies the gore formed by the junction of Front and Wellington Streets. The oblique convergence of two thoroughfares like this resulted in an awkward triangular site, often in a prime commercial location. The builder's solution was to erect a wedge-shaped structure, dubbed a "flat-iron" building for obvious reasons, which made optimum use of the land. William Kauffman, a graduate of a German school of architecture and civil engineering, was the architect. It was built in 1892.

The present building replaced an earlier, blunter flat-iron, the Coffin Block, which housed Toronto's stagecoach depot. Earlier still, it was the site of the city wood market.

The first tenants of the new building, besides Gooderham and Worts, Maltsters, were two insurance agencies and the Montreal Plate Glass Company. Perhaps it was the glass company which supplied the curved glass for the windows in the building's tower. This fanciful medieval turret is a good example of late Victorian taste, a grab-bag of architectural styles executed with modern technology and materials.

The materials of the Gooderham Building are similar to those used in building Upper Canada College two years later and described as "red Credit Valley sandstone ... red pressed brick ... with terra cotta panels and string courses."[1] These types of materials

william Roberts GOODERHAM BUILDING

were manufactured by local firms such as the Don Valley Pressed Bricks Works, the Ontario Terra Cotta and Brick Company, the Toronto Pressed Brick and Terra Cotta Company, "manufacturers of plain, moulded, ornamental, red and coloured pressed brick, roof tile, ridging etc."[2] and M. J. Hynes and Bro., proprietors of the Canadian Terra Cotta Company and Plaster Cast Works which made "terra cotta trimmings and fronts."[3]

William Gooderham arrived in Toronto in 1832 as leader of a group of fifty-four people, mainly relatives — a "modern Joshua,"[4] according to an early account. He and his brother-in-law, James Worts, formed a partnership and opened an account at the Bank of Upper Canada (later to be the De La Salle Institute). Worts had laid the foundations for a windmill on the waterfront at the foot of Trinity Street a year before, but the windmill was not ready for operation until the fall of 1832. From then until the end of the year, 2,991 bushels of wheat, at an average cost of 93 cents per bushel, were ground into 293 barrels of flour. The first recorded sale from the new mill was to Robert Ferrier, a King Street baker, on October 27, 1832.

For its first five years the mill made only flour. Then it became involved, inadvertently as it were, in converting grain into alcohol. A somewhat apologetic account records the transition:

> The addition of a distillery was only a minor consideration at the time this branch was established. During the operation of flourmaking, a large amount of waste grain, siftings, etc., had to be disposed of and its conversion into alcohol was the readiest means to accomplish this object, the ready sale of the beverage which at that time was considered almost as one of the necessities of life, and the exceeding small duty exacted by the Government decided the establishing of a distillery plant which came into active operation in 1837, and in the course of time resulted in a large industry that produced goods of the highest reputation.[5]

The new enterprise flourished; thirty years later it employed 160 workers and turned out 7,500 gallons of whiskey annually. The Gooderhams prospered and William Gooderham's generosity and organizational ability were actively employed in the building, in 1843-44, of Trinity Church on King Street.

As the company grew, there also grew a tendency to question the status of its product as "almost one of the necessities of life." Opposition to alcohol gradually gained ground. *Ten Nights in a Bar-Room* by T. S. Arthur sold ten thousand copies within a month of its publication in 1854 and inspired the pathetic song, *Come Home, Father*, by Henry Work. Noah Webster's *Elementary Spelling Book* for school use included in its practice sentences such editorial comments as:

> Intemperance is the grievous sin of our country. Liquors that intoxicate

are to be avoided as poison. Drunkards are worthless fellows, and despised. The drunkard's course is progressive; he begins by drinking a little, and shortens his life by drinking to excess.

This last sentiment was firmly believed by the Temperance and General Life Assurance Company which gave total abstainers "the full benefit of their more favourable mortality."[6] Non-drinkers could eat at the Toronto Temperance Restaurant and Dining Hall in the Grand Opera Building on Adelaide Street West ("best dinner in the city, at 20 cents")[7]. Obviously, drinking in restaurants was the normal state of affairs, if a restaurant had to advertise its absence.

Although the temperance movement effectively curtailed public drinking habits and the number of outlets for the purchase of liquor, it did not greatly affect a large distillery such as Gooderham and Worts. Any losses suffered during Canada's prohibition era (roughly between 1916 and 1927; it varied according to province) were recouped during the United States' prohibition, a period which proved to be a boon to Canadian brewers and distillers.

Massey Hall

Massey Hall, at the corner of Victoria and Shuter Streets, opened on June 14, 1894, a gift to the people of Toronto from Hart Massey. Its stated purpose was "to encourage or assist the musical, educational, or industrial advancement of the people, the promotion of the cause of temperance, the cultivation of good citizenship…through public and other meetings."[8]

Although it is doubtful whether any one building could satisfy all these requirements, one of its purposes has been fulfilled over the years — that of musical advancement. The original name inscribed over the entrance doors was "Massey Music Hall," but the later addition of a fire door has obliterated part of the word Music. In general, these later concessions to safety have not enhanced the hall's appearance.

Vincent Massey, Hart's grandson, who laid the foundation stone of the hall when he was six years old, says in his memoirs: "Despite its unlovely architecture, it has contributed much to the development of music in Canada."[9] Massey Hall has served as Toronto's pre-eminent concert hall for most of the twentieth century. It is home to the Toronto Symphony Orchestra, the Mendelssohn Choir, and is host to virtually every musician of international stature who performs in Toronto. Designed by architect G. M. Miller, it seats almost three thousand.

William Roberts   MASSEY HALL

Hart Massey was the son of Daniel Massey, the founder of the farm machinery company which bears the Massey name. Both during his lifetime and after (through the Massey Foundation), Hart Massey made many public endowments — the Fred Victor Mission, Massey Hall, and Hart House at the University of Toronto are but a few.

Hart had two famous grandsons — Vincent and Raymond. Both performed at Hart House theatre; Raymond has had a long and illustrious career in the theatre. Vincent went into government service and became Canada's first native-born governor general.

Massey Hall has a well-deserved reputation for superb acoustics. (According to a man in the box office, everything else is wrong *but* the acoustics.) This is no small achievement when one notes that a hall built as recently as 1962 — Avery Hall in Lincoln Centre, New York — in 1976 had to undergo massive reconstruction to make it acoustically satisfactory.

The first concert hall built with the aid of acoustical planners was Symphony Hall in Boston in 1900. The consultant was a Harvard professor in the physics faculty, Wallace

Sabine, who acted as adviser to the hall's chief architect, Charles McKim. Prior to that time good acoustics had depended mainly on luck or the right instinct of the architect.

What of Vincent Massey's charge of unlovely architecture? It *is* plain and unpretentious according to then prevailing standards of taste and, despite touches such as Moorish arches and stained glass windows, the hall is spare, undecorated, utilitarian red brick. But it suits its donor — a solid and practical structure dedicated to culture and the public good by a serious, industrious, and highminded man. As his grandson Raymond said: "All through his life Hart Massey remained a Puritan, guided by the Ten Commandments . . . not one of which he ever broke."[10]

To such a man, utility was more important than appearance, and, by today's standards, Massey Hall is generally considered ugly but useful. A recent study acknowledges its inadequacies and proposes several solutions, one of which involves its renovation and the redevelopment of much of the city block adjacent to it. In the meantime, the old "unlovely" hall keeps on working through its eighty-fourth year.

Bank of Montreal

The Bank of Montreal was the city's first commercial bank. It was established in Toronto in 1818, originally as the Bank of the People. In 1842 that name was changed to the Bank of Montreal and in 1845 its offices were moved to the corner of Yonge and Front Streets. The present bank replaces an earlier building designed by Kivas Tully, a noted Toronto architect.

This impressive building, completed in 1886, was described at the time as "an edifice magnificent in every respect ... without exception the finest designed bank in the Dominion."[11] Despite the unfortunate modernization of the front doors, the structure remains everything a bank should be—substantial, imposing, monumental—of the sort to rattle a Stephen Leacock, a building to inspire confidence that one's funds, however meagre, are cossetted in absolute security.

According to contemporary accounts, the architectural style was "French Renaissance,"[12] or "the composite order of architecture in which the Corinthian predominates,"[13] but while it was a "new departure in its style and character in this country, it is one which must recommend itself even to the critic."[14]

Architects Darling and Curry were responsible for the design, which was realized at a cost of $125,000.

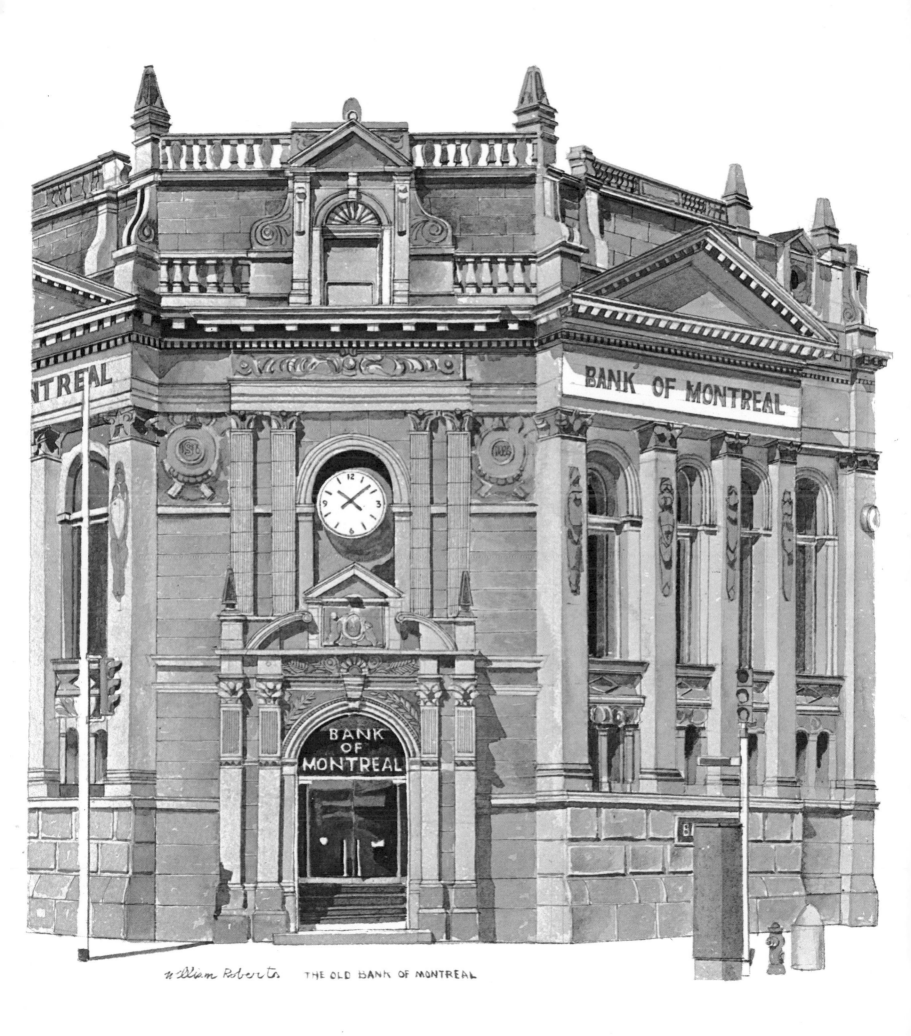

BANK OF MONTREAL

BANK
OF
MONTREAL

William Roberts   THE OLD BANK OF MONTREAL

The building inspired reporters to heights of unbridled enthusiasm, excessive even for those effusive times. Given the Victorian penchant for symbolism, the exterior ornamentation is described, not surprisingly, in this way:

> The pilasters . . . are richly sculptured, the designs, surmounted by mask heads, emblematic of various subjects. On the south are (1) Commerce (2) Music (3) Architecture (4) Agriculture. On the east front are (1) Industry (2) Science (3) Literature (4) Arts; and over the main entrance are the arms of the Bank of Montreal. This splendid work has been executed by Messrs. Holbrook and Mollington, architectural sculptors.[15]

From contemporary trade directories we know a good deal about the building techniques and the men who built the bank. The following excerpt is from *Industries of Canada*, 1886:

> Mr. Lionel Yorke, the extensive builder, of this city, was entrusted with the contract of erection, the execution of which amply sustains his already high reputation as a builder. The ceiling which in richness and elaboration is different from any other in the Dominion, was designed and executed by Messrs. M. J. Hynes and Bro. of Toronto. The foundation of the fresco work is on wire cloth corrugated lathing. The pattern is octagonal, and the main ceiling supporting the principals forms a cob-web design, which is thoroughly interlaced with all the mouldings intersecting, of three different sizes, and carrying in each about seven enrichments. The main cornice is hung, as well as the mouldings, in corrugated iron laths, having about thirteen enrichments, set off with a magnificent frieze about eighteen inches in depth. The walls, which are covered with lancrusta-walton, are finished in trowelled stucco, and anything finer of the kind it would be difficult to find anywhere. . . . The material used by Messrs. Hynes and Bro. was all Canadian, and the designs were executed at their warehouse, No. 88 York Street, and then placed in position in the bank. Mr. R. J. Hovendon, to whom was entrusted the fresco painting, has discharged his portion of the work in an equally creditable manner. The ceiling and walls, which are striking and effective, are done in warm yellow, reds, bronze, and gold. The colours are appropriate and harmonize with the variegated reflex light of the spendid dome, which in artistic design and completeness of finish there is nothing finer on this continent. This dome, which is one of the main features of the building, was executed by Messrs. J. McCausland & Son of this city. It is divided into eight sections with minor subdivisions. The design, which is a peculiarly striking one, embodies an allegorical treat-

ment of the guardian of the gold, in which an eagle is represented as in the act of clutching the gold, while another animal of huge proportions, with two great tails and not belonging strictly to any genus of zoology, defends it. These animals are supported on the main scroll in the Italian Renaissance style. In the centre there are eight circles containing emblems of the Provinces of the Dominion, and the outer panel is chastely festooned with beautiful fruits and flowers, on an architectural background. The colours are striking and effective, and when one enters the Bank of Montreal, instead of looking straight before one as is usually the case, one's eyes are immediately raised to the ceiling.

Ah, the glory that was banking!

Post Office

When the Seventh Post Office at 10 Toronto Street was completed in 1853, *The Globe* reported:

> The provisions for the accommodation of the public, in beauty of design and practical convenience, far surpass anything we have seen in North America, and do great credit to the architect, Mr. Cumberland.

The Globe account failed to give equal credit to William Storm, a former pupil of William Thomas, the architect who built St. Lawrence Hall. Storm had joined Colonel Frederick Cumberland's firm in 1850 and was made a partner in 1852. Their association continued until 1865; together they designed many of Toronto's more notable civic and residential buildings.

This substantial, handsome structure was said at the time to have been patterned upon the Temple of Minerva, just as the St. Lawrence Hall was modelled on another temple, that of Jupiter Stator.

The Victorians regarded their own era with abundant optimism, as the culmination of the entire progress of civilization. They regarded the past with respect rather than awe, since they could re-create the greatest achievements of former ages, improved by modern technology and enhanced by the moral dimension of utility.

William Roberts THE OLD POST OFFICE

The Handbook of Toronto, 1858, describes the Post Office as:

> A very fine specimen of Grecian architecture. It is a chaste and elegant building, with a Greek Ionic front of free stone, with massive fluted columns supporting a bold entablature, on which is cut in *alto relievo* the words POST OFFICE. The whole is surmounted by the Royal Arms, very boldly and neatly sculptured. The building occupies a lot fifty-four feet in front by ninety-six feet in depth, and stands detached, having a carriage way all around. The public hall is forty-four feet by eighteen feet, paved with large flagstones from Ogdensburgh. It has two entrances on Toronto Street and is lighted by windows at the ends and in the front.

The account goes on to say there were 1149 "pigeon holes" or private boxes for which was charged a fee of seven shillings and sixpence a year. Furthermore, the keys to these boxes were individually unique and not interchangeable, "thus affording security as well as convenience."[16]

The second floor, accessible from a private entrance on the south side, provided accommodation for the Post Office Inspector and his assistants and contained a bathroom and water closets. In the basement were living quarters for the porter and messenger, as well as the furnace and fuel rooms. "The whole building is heated by one of Chilson's Hot

Air Furnaces and is well lighted with gas and supplied with an abundance of water, having hydrants on each floor with a sufficient quantity of hose pipe and branches to pour a copious stream of water into every room at a moment's notice."[17]

All this at a cost of £3,500 (roughly $16,000)!

Around 1850 the mail was delivered from England once every two weeks; in winter by stage coach from Halifax and in summer partly by steamboat. The postage rate on a letter sent from Toronto to Halifax was two shillings and ninepence. Postage stamps were not then in use; rather, the charge was written in red ink on prepaid letters, in black ink on unpaid letters. In 1852 control of the postal service was transferred from the Imperial government to the Canadian government, and, with the cooperation of the United States, mails began to arrive weekly via Boston and New York.

The Seventh Post Office was in use less than twenty years for its original purpose. Toronto's rapid growth required larger postal facilities and the Eighth Post Office, huge in comparison and unmistakably Victorian in design, was built at the head of Toronto Street in 1872 to 1873. By 1886 there were, in addition, three branch offices and daily mail delivery was anticipated.

In 1959 the old post office was bought by the Argus Corporation to serve as the company's head office. It was thus saved from probable destruction, and the company is to be commended for the taste and judgment with which the building has been preserved.

St. Lawrence Hall

The St. Lawrence Hall derives its name from the city ward in which it stands. When York was incorporated in 1834 as the city of Toronto, it was divided into five wards: St. Patrick's, St. Andrew's, St. David's, St. George's, and St. Lawrence — names which reflect the origins of the early colonists.

Two of the other wards also had their own markets: St. Patrick's, Queen Street West, south of the Grange, on land donated by D'Arcy Boulton, and St. Andrew's, on "Little Richmond" Street, one block west of Spadina and one block south of Queen. But the St. Lawrence was the oldest and largest market, having been on that site since the earliest days of York. The area was officially designated as the Market Square by proclamation in 1803. It contained the public pillory and stocks and a communal well and pump, besides the usual market fare. During the fire of 1849, the King Street front of the existing market building was damaged so badly that it had to be razed.

The present hall was designed by William Thomas and constructed during 1850-51 at a cost of slightly over $28,000. The painting shows the west side of the hall. The sides and back are constructed principally of brick, whereas the King Street façade is entirely of cut stone, a fairly common nineteenth century building treatment. Such a structure was described as having a "Lady Anne front and a Mary Anne back" — the latter being a popular name among Irish servant girls.

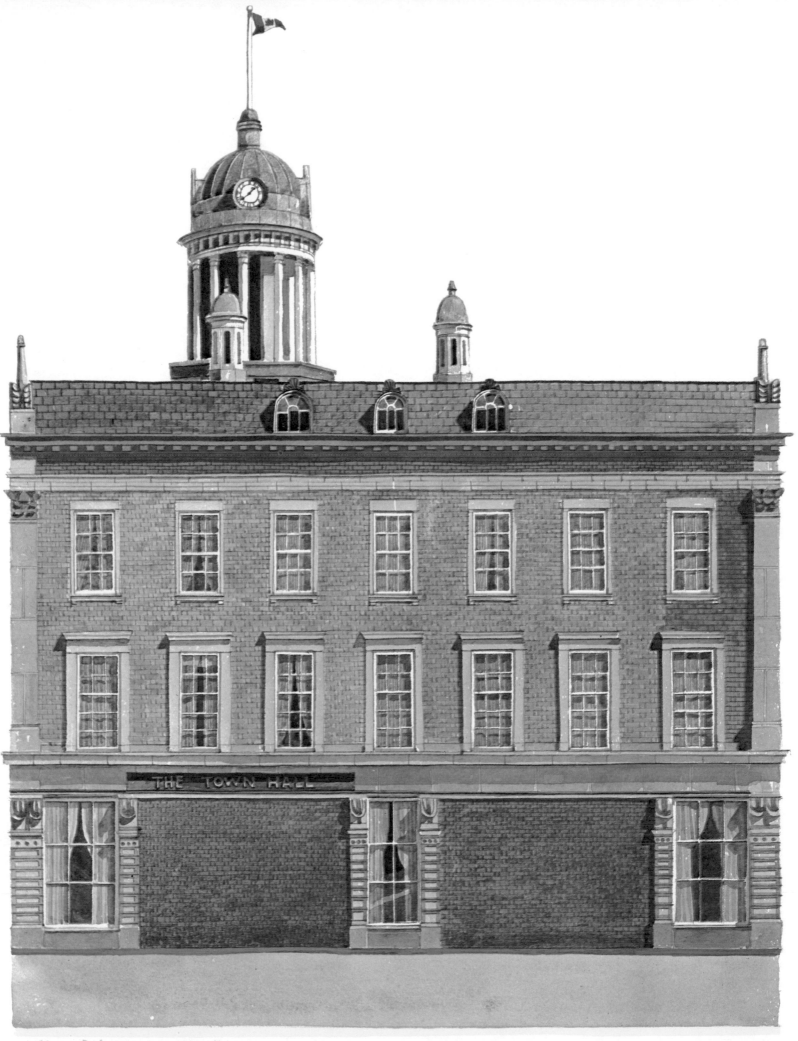

THE TOWN HALL

William R. Abbott ST. LAWRENCE HALL

In early references, the St. Lawrence Hall was usually called a Market-hall, a term which gives a clearer concept of the range of the hall's uses—cultural, social, educational, and commercial. Inside the building at street level was an arcade of shops opening on to an interior corridor. The floor plan of the building is a central rectangle flanked by two square wings. The King Street façade is flush, so that the larger centre block extended into the Market Square at the rear of the building. This section was given over to butchers' stalls which opened both into the hall and out to the Market Square. Present-day nature conservationists will be appalled to learn that these stalls occasionally sold wild turkeys and the "rare wild swan,"[18] as well as common domestic meat and fowl.

In 1850, shortly before the building was completed, the leases on the small shops were sold at auction. Annual rents ranged from a low of £20 to a high of £81, depending on size, location, and storage facilities. Of the thirteen successful bidders, most sold fancy wares and confectionery. One sold books.

The hall also contained assembly rooms for various patriotic and benevolent societies and a Commercial Reading Room. But it was the Great Hall on the third floor, "very lofty and large and beautifully lighted,"[19] according to an early patron, which was the scene of the most fashionable balls, soirées, suppers, promenades, musicales, and concerts held in Toronto between 1851 and 1870.

Seating a thousand people, it was reputedly free of echoes. Entertainers as diverse as Tom Thumb and Jenny Lind performed here under the sponsorship of impresario P. T. Barnum. Jenny Lind's 1851 concert has achieved the status of legend. It also served as a hall for lectures on such current topics as the rights of women, the abolition of slavery, and the temperance movement. Politicians of every stripe held meetings here, as did fund-raisers for many worthy causes.

During the 1870s the popularity of the hall for entertainments began to be eclipsed by the erection of other concert and assembly halls and a growth pattern which moved the town centre farther to the northwest. At the end of the century it was reduced mainly to market and commercial use. No longer were fancy wares sold—the stall sellers were listed simply as "hucksters."

In 1967, however, the old hall experienced a renaissance when the city of Toronto, as a centennial project, restored it to its former grace and grandeur under the supervision of architect Eric Arthur.

All Saints' Church

In 1872, when the neighbourhood around Sherbourne and Dundas Streets was a new residential area, a group of Anglicans purchased the site at the southeast corner for $2,200. The first church they built was a small wooden building which soon proved inadequate, so that in 1874 a substantial brick church was built at a cost of $15,000 to the design of architects Windeyer and Falloon.

All Saints' is built in the manner of an early English parish church, retaining the simplicity but lacking the austerity of that style. Proportions are on a human scale; it sits comfortably on its site and its lines are squatter than the soaring Gothic of the downtown cathedrals. Its appearance is deceptive, as it seems to be a small church, but it is actually spacious — with a full complement of pews, it could accommodate a congregation of eight hundred.

The most conspicuous feature is the use of two colours of brick, red and yellow, laid in a geometric design and used to emphasize architectural details. The brick patterns and the comfortable proportions combine to give it warmth and friendliness — appropriately so, as today the church has an open door policy, serving as a drop-in centre and ministering to the varied needs of the community.

William Roberts ALL SAINTS CHURCH

With a few exceptions, the Gothic or "pointed" style was preferred for ecclesiastical buildings in the nineteenth century.

> In the forms of the Gothic cathedral are embodied the worshipping principle, the loving reverence for that which is highest, and the sentiment of Christian brotherhood, or that perception of affiliation which is founded on recognizing in man goodness and truth, and reverencing them in him. This is expressed in the principal lines, which are all vertical (aspiring, tending upward); in the whole mass falling under, or within the pyramidal (the fire, or symbol of love) form; in the pointed character of all the openings, *ogive*, as the French call it, being the ideal line expressive of firmness of base, embracingness of tendency, and upward ascension as its ultimate aim; and in the clustering and grouping of its multiple parts. Gothic architecture being thus representative rather of the Unity of Love, than of the Diversities of Faith, it seems proper that it should be the style used for all ecclesiastical and other purposes having reference to religious life.[20]

Without subscribing to all the notions of this heavy-handed symbolism, we can

approve the attitudes exalted—the ideals of Christian brotherhood and charity. It must be noted that these high-falutin' Victorian words expressed sentiments in accord with the practical Christianity of the present-day ministry of All Saints', concerned as it is with the "Unity of Love" rather than the "Diversities of Faith." Reverend Norman Ellis, rector of All Saints' since 1964, recounts in his delightful book, *My Parish Is Revolting*, how All Saints' changed from a parish for a middle-class community to an active downtown social centre for "skid row." The church buildings are now used to their fullest capacity in ways unimagined in the genteel days of the parish.

One advantage of the church's open door, aside from the cheap and good coffee, is that a visitor interested in buildings can go inside at any time. Gazing out from the stained glass windows are lovely pre-Raphaelite faces posing as Biblical characters. Richly colourful tiles form the floor of the chancel behind an ornate brass lectern surmounted by a large eagle. But the most remarkable spectacle, and one indicative of the new All Saints', occurred in the busy parish hall on a recent weekday afternoon. One old man was playing cards with manifest enjoyment. Each time he slapped down a winning card, he would gleefully shout, "F.....g lovely!"

Nobody flinched.

Campbell House

This neo-classical Georgian manor house was built by Sir William Campbell in 1822. Toronto historian Henry Scadding called it "a mansion of brick in good style."[21] Its original site was on the north side of Duke Street (now Adelaide Street East) at the head of Frederick Street, and afforded a view of the bay.

Sir William Campbell was Chief Justice of Upper Canada from 1825 to 1829. On his retirement he was knighted, the first Canadian judge to be so honoured. In 1972 the Advocates' Society, a society of courtroom lawyers practising in Ontario, bought Campbell House and moved it to the northwest corner of University Avenue and Queen Street, where it now stands.

The house has been restored at great cost and is now open to the public. In the restoration, any suggestion of what the English painter, John Piper, termed "pleasing decay" has been ruthlessly eliminated. So antiseptic and naked is the appearance of the exterior, that it recalls Mrs. Anna Jameson's 1836 reference to the "staring red brick"[22] of Toronto buildings. Any qualities for which old buildings are prized, such as the mellowness and dignity of age, are sadly lacking.

William Roberts   THE CAMPBELL HOUSE

William Campbell was born in Scotland in 1758. He enlisted in a Highland regiment during the American Revolutionary War, was posted to America, and served under General Cornwallis. At the Battle of Yorktown in 1781 he was captured, together with his regiment. He was released two years later when peace was declared and went to live in Nova Scotia. There he studied law and, after nineteen years' practice, was appointed Attorney General of Cape Breton. In 1811 he was promoted to a judgeship in Upper Canada.

Campbell was sixty-six years old when appointed Chief Justice. It was said that his appointment was an interim one, that his role was to keep the bench warm for John Beverley Robinson, then Attorney-General, who was too young to be a Chief Justice.

A well-known lawsuit, which the new Chief Justice heard, was the civil action arising out of the raid on the office of the *Colonial Advocate*, William Lyon Mackenzie's newspaper. This outrage, perpetrated in broad daylight in full view of two British magistrates, did not warrant a criminal charge in Upper Canada in 1826, and Mackenzie had to press a civil suit for damages. These were granted by Chief Justice Campbell and a special jury, to the amount of $2,500. Among the defendants were two sons of the Inspector-General, a son of a judge, the confidential secretary of the Lieutenant Governor, and other young bloods of good family.

Whether Campbell's conduct of the case is to be construed as a mark of his integrity and sterling character is questionable. The recorded facts constitute an apparently open and shut case, and, even though the verdict went against the reigning powers, public sympathy was with Mackenzie, strong enough to send him to the Legislature in 1828.

Just a century later this "mansion of brick in good style" suffered the ravages of rooming house tenants, and in 1930 it became a nail factory. Its original interior was at that time either removed or drastically altered. Eric Arthur says it suffered the "indignity of evisceration."[23] But perhaps the greater indignity to the old house is to present it as a shoddy parody of its former elegance. John Ruskin called this sort of restoration being "scraped and patched up into smugness and smoothness more tragic than uttermost ruin."[24]

National Hotel

Probably built between 1876 and 1877, the National Hotel replaced two three-storey brick buildings which stood on the site and were listed in the 1857 assessment rolls as "unfinished houses" owned by George Ross. When completed in 1861, the house on the corner was rented to Francis Sullivan, a grocer, for $184 a year. George Ross kept the second house and ran it as an inn. Ross had been on this corner of King Street East and Sherbourne (then Caroline) Street a full decade earlier, running an establishment which went by the grandiose name of the British Exchange Inn.

During the 1860s the corner building was a grocery and the second building a saloon. John Terry, a flour dealer, operated a business just down King Street a few steps from the hotel. In 1871 he set up his flour, feed, and delivery service on this corner. By 1874 he had moved his parcel delivery to Adelaide Street East and converted the corner property to a hotel and a Museum of Canadian Curiosities. Unfortunately, this imaginative enterprise did not catch on with the public and lasted only a few years.

The present hotel, completed by 1878 and managed by William Burke, was first known as the Grand Central. The name National Hotel did not appear until 1899. It remained the National until the late 1960s. The rear wall still bears the name in faded paint.

william Roberts THE OLD NATIONAL HOTEL

This corner at King and Sherbourne has always been a favourite location for a tavern, although, with the nineteenth century's predilection for strong drink, this could be said of almost any corner of old Toronto. Six years before George Ross's British Exchange Inn of 1850, there was a saloon at or very near this corner first run by S. Stroud and two years later by John Wright. Not far from here stood M. Whitemore's saloon, with the wonderful name of Live and Let Live Tavern.

There was never any shortage of tippling houses in the neighbourhood. In 1864 fourteen buildings stood on the south side of King Street in the two blocks between Frederick and Princess Streets. Of these, six were saloons. Patrick Sheady kept a tavern here and John Law's tavern, a year later, had the added attraction of a "ball alley."

The term "hotel" or "inn" was applied loosely in those days as there was no set number of rooms the hotel keeper had to rent which entitled him to the use of the word. But as the temperance movement gained ground in the province and the city, further liquor restrictions were enacted with particular emphasis on the more stringent regulation of tavern licences and the obligation to provide rooms for the travelling public in order to qualify for a liquor licence. These processes of the law effectively put the small corner store type of saloon out of business, while the tavern-hotel was able to survive even the later period of prohibition.

Even these concessions did not satisfy avid temperance advocates, as this poem from the 1880s illustrates:

Low Grog Shops v. Fashionable Saloons

The Devil grows aristocratic of late,
And he wants a house more grand,
So down goes the wooden shanty,
To make room for a stylish stand,
He has dealt out death to thousands,
And it reaped him a harvest fair;
To prove how the work has paid,
A costly house he'll rear.

He will build it of bricks that were purchased
With the drunkard's pains and fears;
He will fit it with gleaming windows
That are made of frozen tears,
And the money that at his counter
Made a father's brain grow wild,
Till he beat an invalid woman,
And killed his beautiful child.

48

Come, hasten, ye merry masons,
Build up the towering wall,
Work well, work fast, good fellows,
You shall be paid for all.
Paid in the drunkard's money,
Which left his wife unfed,
And sent his children weeping,
Hungry and cold to bed.

Pull down the old frame building!
Make room for a new one here!
For this dear homes were mortgaged,
Or sold by the auctioneer.
No matter if little children
Stay homeless through the land,
Down with the old frame building,
Make room for the stylish stand![25]

In the 1890s a hotel like the National would rent a room for about $1.50 a night, while the big hostelries such as the Rossin House and Queen's charged $3.00 to $4.50.

Over the past one hundred years the National has had many owners and managers. One, Charles Brewer, who christened it the National, kept it for ten years around the turn of the century, but the longest tenure was that of George Merrydew, who owned it for thirty years from the 1920s until the 1950s.

Mackenzie House

Mackenzie House at 82 Bond Street, originally the central house of a row of three, is a fine example of a Georgian town house, built around 1850. It was the home, during the last years of his life, of William Lyon Mackenzie, the first mayor of Toronto.

The house was saved from demolition in 1936 by T. Wilbur Best, who established a foundation to refurbish it as a museum and library. In 1960 ownership was transferred to the city of Toronto.

The Toronto Historical Board has restored Mackenzie House to its mid-nineteenth century condition, incorporating many personal possessions of the Mackenzie family. A wing added to the back contains a reconstruction of the printing shop which Mackenzie used so effectively to harass the ruling forces of the day.

Mackenzie House has a wonderful atmosphere of shabby gentility entirely in keeping with the family's reduced circumstances. In 1859 it had been purchased for £950 through the generosity of friends, and presented to Mackenzie "as a mark of esteem and in recognition of his public services."[26] But already he was in failing health and he died here in 1861.

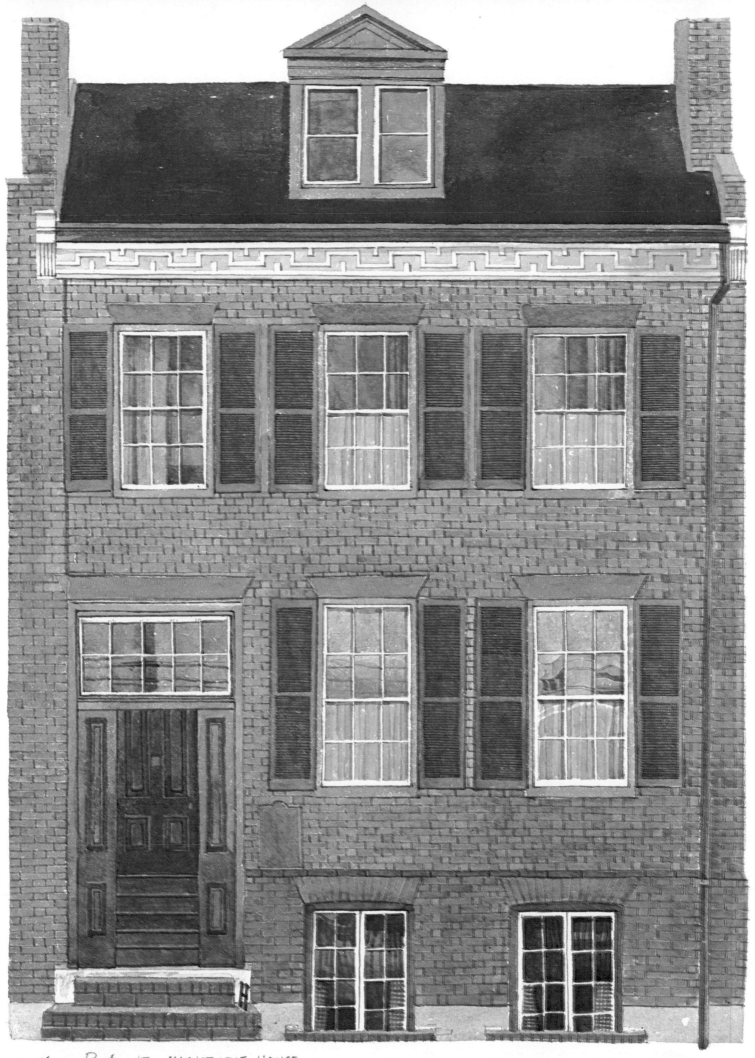

william Roberts MACKENZIE HOUSE

William Lyon Mackenzie, reformer and rebel, was instrumental in effecting permanent political change in Canada. He arrived in this country from his native Scotland in 1820 and established two businesses—in York in that year and, in 1822, in Dundas. Two years later he moved to Queenston and began to publish his controversial newspaper, the *Colonial Advocate.* Shortly thereafter, however, he returned to York, the provincial capital.

Here, through his newspaper, he resumed his attacks on the ruling oligarchy in Upper Canada, the Family Compact, who were attempting to govern the province as a private club. So effective were Mackenzie's diatribes that in 1826 several relatives and close associates of the Attorney General and administrative officials raided the King Street offices of the *Colonial Advocate*, demolished them, and threw the type in the bay— in the presence of two British magistrates!

Mackenzie did not miss this opportunity to capitalize on the situation morally and politically and was inspired to new heights in fiery journalism. Public sympathy was aroused and Mackenzie was elected to the Assembly of Upper Canada in 1828. His opposition to the government did not lessen, and he was repeatedly ejected from the Legislature and ultimately denied a seat.

Mackenzie was a flamboyant man with inflammatory views. He had lost his hair as a result of a childhood fever and wore a flaming red wig. He used the wig with effect to punctuate his moods — throwing it up in elation or down in rage.

In 1834 Mackenzie was elected alderman of the newly incorporated city of Toronto and chosen by his fellow aldermen as first mayor. The city's coat of arms is reputed to be his design. He was not, however, re-elected to another term, nor were he and his fellow Reform Party candidates successful in the provincial elections of 1836, with the outcome that Mackenzie and his followers moved into closer alliance with their rebellious counterparts in Lower Canada. Eventually their dissatisfaction culminated in the disastrous Rebellion of 1837; Mackenzie and his family were obliged to spend the next twelve years in exile in the United States.

In 1849 a general amnesty was granted by the Canadian Government, and the family returned to Toronto. Once again Mackenzie became involved in provincial politics, when in 1851 he was elected to represent Haldimand County. Two years later he was back in the publishing business with his last newspaper, *Mackenzie's Weekly Message.* He retired from politics in 1858 and from publishing in 1860.

His behaviour had become more erratic, his temperament more irascible, his financial affairs more improvident, but, due to the kindness of his friends, he was able to die, in 1861, in some degree of comfort and security in his own house on Bond Street.

Dominion Brewery

For more than fifty years the building at 496 Queen Street East, now abandoned, was the office of the Dominion Brewery, Brewers, Maltsters, and Bottlers. The brewing works extended to the west, while the conveniently located Dominion Hotel was to the east. Presumably, the hotel served Dominion beer.

The only changes in the appearance of the building, aside from its derelict condition, have been in the top storey. The large central window was originally circular with ornamental glazing; the small side dormers had curved tops. One feature of late Victorian architectural design, which seems particularly pointless and ugly, is the truncated tower crowning the front. This was a very familiar device on mansard roofs— De La Salle Institute and 42 Yonge Street have a similar treatment. At best, these towers manqué were surmounted by a rather disproportionate flagpole, when, in fact, they appear to be the first stage of a steeple which lacks its complementary spire.

Whatever their aesthetic failings, the offices apparently were adequate for their administrative function. A photograph from the early 1930s shows a very well-kept, prosperous factory complex, described as "one of the largest in the Dominion of Canada."[27] A few years later, during World War II, the plant was being used to

william Roberts THE OLD DOMINION BREWERY OFFICE

manufacture tires, and the Dominion Brewing Company had seemingly vanished. The buildings, however, remain.

The Dominion Brewery on Queen Street East, founded by Robert Davies, was built in 1879 to 1880. Probably Davies had previously been a partner with his brother Thomas in the Davies Brewing and Malting Company, located one block east on Queen Street at the corner of River Street. Before the Dominion Brewery was started, the Davies Brewery was owned by Thomas Davies and Brother, but afterwards there was no mention of a brother. For a time during the 1860s the older brewery was called the Don Brewery, taking its name from the nearby river.

The adjacent Dominion Hotel, built in 1889 at the corner of Sumach Street, continues to operate as a tavern. It was first managed by G. Hale. Both the brewery and the hotel flourished in this area of the city, locally known as Corktown. Corktown took its name from the Freyseng Cork Company situated across the intersection on Sumach Street, where it had been a fixture in the neighbourhood since 1885. As the cork works manufactured "corks, bungs, and bottle baskets,"[28] it is probable they supplied the brewery with these items.

It is equally probable that the two companies were the major employers of those who lived in the area. Many of the semi-detached houses and cottages in the surrounding streets date from the 1880s. With three churches and a school within a two-block radius and the ubiquitous corner grocery stores, Corktown was a fairly self-sufficient community.

It is a matter of some curiosity how brewers and distillers survived the era of prohibition which, in Canada, was euphemistically called temperance. The Canada Temperance Act of 1878 gave municipalities the right to vote themselves wet or dry. This was "local option" and many counties and towns throughout the country went dry. As an emergency wartime measure, prohibition was in effect during World War I and this helped to strengthen the temperance argument. In fact, in 1916, the Ontario Temperance Act became law. This act curtailed the sale of alcohol within the province, except for "sacramental, industrial, artistic, mechanical, scientific, and medicinal purposes." In other words, alcohol was not to be drunk except in very rare and unusual circumstances.

These circumstances included religion (sacramental purposes) and health — in the case of health, under a doctor's prescription in minimum quantities, not exceeding six ounces. One aspect, which the official brewing industry accounts of the period completely ignore, is the phenomenon known as "near beer"—a beverage sometimes called "temperance beer" containing approximately 2.5 percent alcohol, which was considered non-intoxicating under the Ontario Temperance Act. Hotels could sell this ersatz brew with cigars, cigarettes, and ice-cream, if licensed to do so.

Apparently the only way to make near beer is first to make real beer and then remove some of the alcohol. It is reasonable to assume that Dominion Brewery was engaged in this activity. Production records of the Canadian brewing industry did not decrease drastically in the period between 1916 and 1927, the period of the Ontario Temperance Act and similar legislation in other provinces. Most of this period coincided with prohibition in the United States, and, while Canadian consumption of alcohol declined to half its previous rate, government revenue from alcohol production in Canada increased by four hundred percent. A logical conclusion is that much of this product found its way to the United States by illicit means.

Whatever factors were responsible for the disappearance of Dominion Brewery — the Depression, business competition, or whatever — the forces of temperance presumably had little to do with it.

Fire Hall

The red brick bastion at 110 Lombard Street is a former firehouse built, as the medallion on the front gable shows, in 1886. In that year there were at least twelve other fire halls in the city, engine houses, hook and ladder companies, and hose stations.

The tall medieval style of tower served a purpose other than as belfry and watch-tower. It acted as a drying room where the wet canvas and rubber hoses were hung.

Electric signal boxes had been installed throughout the city in 1872. Directions for their operation were as follows:

> Keys are left with the occupants of buildings in the vicinity of each fire-alarm box. The members of the police force are also provided with keys. The following course should be followed when a fire is observed: Go to the box, open the door, and pull the hook down as far as it will go, firmly and without jerking; then let it slide back, when the alarm will be immediately heard from the small bell within, and will be followed by that upon the tower bell.[29]

william Roberts OLD CENTRAL FIRE HALL

At the first alarm "the firemen from the stations always turn out with the utmost alacrity, their splendid horses galloping along the streets."[30] A tribute to the Toronto firemen written in 1891 contained this surprising statement:

> Toronto's Fire Brigade vies in efficiency, and may we not say, in no objectionable sense, in the lust of manhood, with the city's other protecting arm, the Police Force.[31]

The first attempts at fire prevention and control in York were under the authority of the provincial government. In 1801 it was decreed that every householder was obliged to:

> Provide and keep Two Buckets for carrying water, when any House shall happen to be on Fire, which buckets shall be made of Wood, Leather, or Canvas, painted on the outside and covered with pitch on the inside, and shall hold, at least, two Gallons of water; and the said Buckets shall be marked with the Christian and Sirname (sic) of the Housekeeper to whose House they belong, and shall not be used for any other purpose than the extinguishing of fires.

Ordered, also

> That every Housekeeper in the said Town, do keep two Ladders, the one to reach from the Ground to the Eaves of the House, and the other to be properly secured and fixed with Hooks or Bolts on the roof near the Chimney.[32]

If an inspection proved that buckets and ladders had not been provided, the householder was liable to a fine of five shillings; if unfortunate enough to have suffered a fire without the prescribed equipment, he was fined forty shillings.

In those early days, with a population of just over three hundred, there was not even an organization of volunteer fire fighters — everyone was expected to help. A fire engine had been donated by the Lieutenant Governor, and, in 1830, £100 was raised annually to support the fire engine and pay for police services. By 1835, however, fire protection seems to have become more businesslike, as the City Council voted a grant of £25 to the Hook and Ladder Company for general expenses and £45 for suitable uniforms.

The city's water supply was inadequate throughout the century and was still a problem in fire emergencies as late as 1884. At mid-century, the licensed carters of the city were required to attend all fires, carrying water from the bay in casks. There was a reward of two dollars for the carter first on the scene, and it is reported that they usually filled up their casks in the evening and took them home to be ready in case of need.

In 1850 the fire brigade consisted of four engine companies, two hook and ladder companies, and one hose company under the leadership of James Ashfield, chief engineer. The chief, and later an assistant, were paid, permanent employees; volunteers were paid an annual retaining fee, reimbursed for fires attended, but not actually bound to do so. In 1874 a professional department was established with thirty-six men at an initial cost of $12,000 per year. James Ashfield was appointed chief, a position he held until 1889, having served forty years as Toronto's chief firefighter.

The two biggest fires in Toronto's history were in 1849 and 1904. The first destroyed a large area around the Market Square including St. James' Cathedral; the second required the assistance of the Buffalo Fire Department!

The Lombard Street fire hall has now been converted into a restaurant featuring cabaret style entertainment and called, appropriately enough, the Old Firehall. It is hoped that once in a while here, in no objectionable sense, the lust of manhood of bygone days is still celebrated.

De La Salle

In 1806 the property at the corner of George and Adelaide Streets, designated as Lot 6, Town of York, was given to trustees of the Roman Catholic community for the building of a chapel. Fifteen years later, when ready to build, the trustees decided the lot was too small and they applied to the Legislature for permission to sell it. Permission was granted and the site was purchased by the Bank of Upper Canada which built the once elegant building still standing on this corner. Proceeds of the sale were used to purchase the land for St. Paul's Church at Power and Queen Streets. The first St. Paul's, opened in 1824, was located just south of the second larger church built in 1889.

The Bank of Upper Canada collapsed in 1866, and the building was bought by the Christian Brothers. They opened a school for boys, which they called De La Salle Institute. In 1871, as the inscription testifies, they expanded their quarters by building an addition eastward from the former bank. No attempt was made to match the classical lines of the bank building. Rather, the style is Victorian Romanesque, then much in vogue for offices and warehouses.

The school remained here for half a century, just down the street from the old Campbell House. It was re-located during World War I, moving to another historic house, Oaklands, on Farnham Avenue.

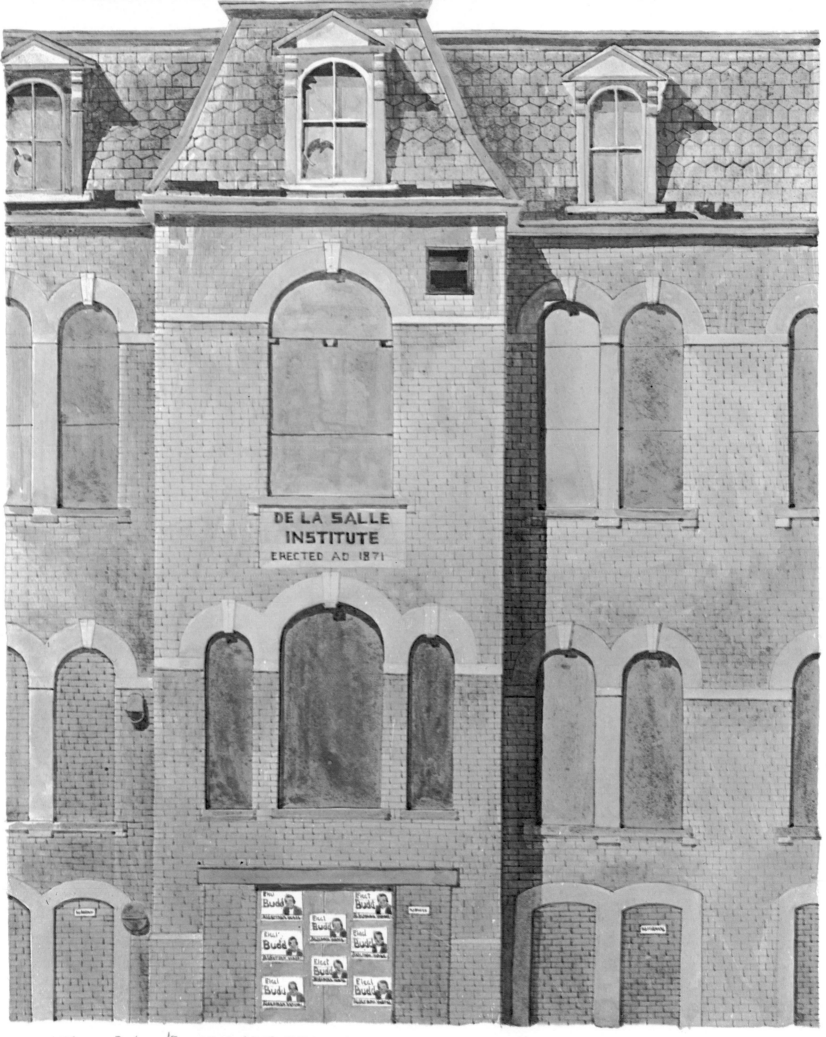

William Roberts DE LA SALLE INSTITUTE

The contribution of the Christian Brothers to education in Toronto pre-dates the establishment of De La Salle. In 1851 five Brothers arrived in Toronto and set up two classes at St. Paul's. Shortly thereafter they started a school in a two-storey frame house on Richmond Street directly behind the Lombard Street fire hall, conducting classes on the ground floor and living upstairs. In 1854 a teaching Brother would receive an annual stipend of £15 — less than $70. At the same time, the smallest shop in the St. Lawrence arcade had an annual rent of £20.

Education in Ontario in the nineteenth century was marked by controversy. Egerton Ryerson, Superintendent of Education for the province from 1844 to 1876, fought to establish the system of free, publicly supported elementary and secondary schools which now exists. Although a Methodist, Ryerson administered fairly the law safeguarding the right of Roman Catholics to have separate schools. De La Salle, however, as both private and sectarian, remained outside these controversies.

There was one controversial issue, neither religious, political, nor financial, which has proved the most enduring. As early as 1832 Dr. Thomas Rolph was speaking out against the deleterious effects of American teachers and textbooks in the schools of Upper Canada. He attacked the texts which gave "false accounts of the late war — geography setting forth New York, Philadelphia, and Boston as the largest and finest cities in the world." He objected to history books "describing the American population as the most free and enlightened under heaven ... American spelling books, dictionary, and grammar, teaching an anti-British idiom and dialect."[33] Dr. Rolph's criticisms were well founded. An 1807 *Geography of the World* by Nathaniel Dwight informs us that New Englanders are:

> An industrious and orderly people; economical in their livings and frugal in their expenses, but very liberal when called on for valuable purposes, or by brethren in distress. They are well informed in general; fond of reading, punctual in their observance of the laws; sociable and hospitable to each other and to strangers; jealous and watchful over their liberties; almost every individual pursuing some gainful and useful calling. They are humane and friendly, wishing well to the human race. They are plain and simple in their manners and, on the whole, they form perhaps the most pleasing and happy society in the world.

The same text reports that Canada is:

> Bounded on the north by New Britain, on the east by the bay of St. Lawrence, on the south by Nova Scotia and the United States, and on the west by unknown lands. The state of commerce is flourishing and consists of furs and peltry, wheat flour, flax-seed, pot-ash, fish, oil, ginseng, and other medicinal roots.

The most striking feature of contemporary spelling books was not their political content but rather their relentless moral didacticism. *Cobb's Spelling Book*, 1835, contained "Select Sentences, of easy words, calculated to teach children to read and at the same time to infuse into their tender minds some just ideas of their duty and the rudiments of sanctity and virtue." Cobb's speller was not only available in Upper Canada but was actually printed at two locations here, in St. Thomas and St. Catharines.

As Superintendent of Education, Ryerson developed a series of school books published in the 1860s which were no less moralistic than their Yankee predecessors. Neither were they appreciably more Canadian in content. Little scholars were treated to cautionary and uplifting tales, such as *The Truant, The Good Little Girl, The Two Good Boys, The Good Brother and Sister, The Liar and The Truthful Boy, Never Say Fail*, and *Try Again*. Even a story with the cheerful title "The Best Fun" ends with the moral that "the best fun is always found in doing something that is kind and useful."[34]

There was never a suggestion of knowledge for the sake of knowledge, for what was the use of learning if it did not make one *good*? As one of the homilies in Noah Webster's 1857 speller solemnly declared: "The most refined education does not embellish the human character like piety."

42 Yonge Street

Measuring 1,178.3 miles from its starting point at Lake Ontario, north as far as Rainy River, Yonge Street is now officially the longest street in the world, and as such has received the imprimatur of the Guinness Book of Records. In the nineteenth century it gained supremacy as the commercial street, although King Street was the most fashionable avenue. An 1861 geography book helpfully explains: "King and Yonge (yung) Streets are the principal thoroughfares."[35]

Numbers 42, 44, and 46 Yonge Street date from a time that saw Toronto mature as a commercial centre. If one ignores the mansard roofs of 42 and 44, and the decorative window cornices of 44, the buildings below display a definite Georgian influence in their proportions and construction. Possibly these were built during the 1850s and the embellishments and the extra storeys were added later — the style of these improvements suggests the seventies. The corner building, 46 Yonge Street, became a bank around 1880, and it is likely that the renovations to the adjoining buildings had occurred a few years before.

The city's assessment rolls invariably describe all three structures as three-storey brick right up to 1900. While it seems unlikely that the addition of the mansard roof storey to Number 42 and Number 44 occurred later, perhaps such an extension was not regarded as an extra storey for tax purposes.

WELLINGTON SALES

MANUFACTURERS & DESTRIBUTORS
OUTLET CENTRE

FOR SPRING
HAND BAGS
AT
SUPER SAVINGS

MAN'S SHIRTS
3 FOR $10⁰⁰

MANY MORE
SUPER BUYS
INSIDE

DENIM JACKET
BOYS 3-10
$9.95 ea

William Roberts NO. 42 YONGE

One interesting aspect of the improvements is the use of tin mouldings as architraves and decorative panels on the three buildings. These were actually constructed of galvanized iron and could be ordered in a variety of styles to embellish an old building. A Toronto firm which supplied these was Douglas Brothers, "Manufacturers of Galvanized Iron Cornices, Window Caps, etc., 95 Adelaide Street West — leading among the industries of Toronto ... the firm is known as the Toronto Galvanized Iron Cornice Works."[36]

44 Yonge Street

Before 1860, records of Toronto's stores and houses are rather uninformative about exact locations. Forty-two Yonge Street housed a boot and shoe wholesaler in the sixties. Later records, however, show that Number 42 and Number 44 Yonge Street were wholesale dry goods firms. One John Charlesworth supplied "British and foreign dry goods."

In 1885, Number 42 was no longer purveying wholesale dry goods. A new publication from the Grip Publishing Company, *The Battle of Batoche*, was available to the trade at the Toronto News Company, located at 42 Yonge Street. This company retained that address long after the turn of the century.

William Roberts NO. 44 YONGE

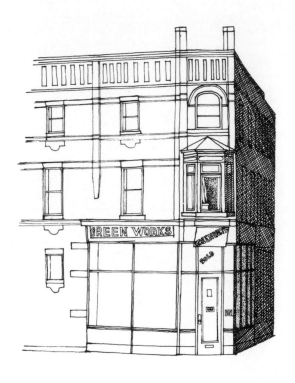

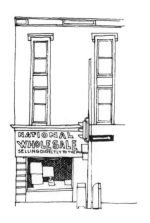

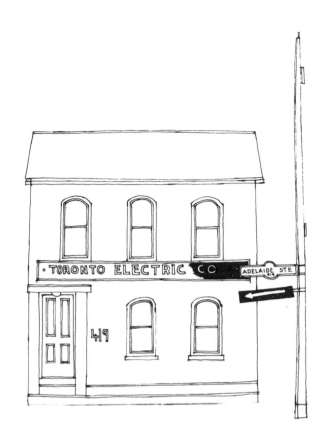

46 Yonge Street

During the 1860s, 46 Yonge Street was a hotel, first called the Argyle Tavern under Duncan McNab, and then the Western Hotel run by Jonathan Mossop, but owned by the Honourable W. P. Howland, postmaster. Title next passed to William Cawthra, meaning that the trio of buildings were by then all owned by a member of the Cawthra family and remained so past the turn of the century.

The Cawthras were leading figures of the Toronto business community throughout the nineteenth century. Their patriarch, Joseph Cawthra, arrived in the town of York before 1800 and set up as a merchant on the northwest corner of King and Sherbourne Streets, across the intersection from the later site of the National Hotel.

After its stint as a hotel, Number 46 was the premises of J. G. Joseph, wholesale jeweller, from 1866 until 1880, when the building became a branch of the Standard Bank. J. L. Brodie, cashier, was in charge. The banking enterprise does not appear to have been successful, as the building reverted to the status of a general merchant's in 1893, run by G. A. Weese.

william Roberts 46 YONGE STREET

Yonge Street's preeminence is well established—the first macadamized road paving in North America in 1833; Toronto's first streetcar line in 1861; its first electric street lamp in 1884.

It is indisputable that Yonge Street is, not just in Toronto but in all those towns through which it travels, Ontario's Main Street.

Mutual Street

Neat, brightly painted houses, small in scale but built with care and fine attention to detail, are united at 63, 65, and 67 Mutual Street. Mansard roofs are slated; decorative keystones are incorporated in the lintels of the doors and windows; half-dormers are trimmed with carved cornices, and over the porches are small, cheerful sun rooms. The terrace was built during the 1880s when Toronto was observing a semi-centennial — fifty years a city.

The occasion was observed with a parade of trades' tableaux. Decorated horse-drawn wagons, displaying merchandise, touted the wares of Toronto industries and merchants. One party was even inspired to form a company in honour of the anniversary — the Semi-Centennial Manufacturing Company, 57 Queen Street East. Its sole product, was "Semi-centennial Bitters . . . No Fraud, No Humbug, But Finest Herbal Bitters In The Market. For Dyspepsia, Sick Headache, Nausea . . ."[37]

In its first fifty years as a city, Toronto's population had increased from 9,254 to 105,000. Few Toronto businesses, however, were equipped with telephone communication. Instead, Torontonians were linked by thirty miles of streetcar tracks with horse-drawn cars, as electric cars were not introduced until 1891. A resident of Mutual

william Roberts MUTUAL ST. ROW HOUSES

Street could board a car on Queen Street, pay a 5-cent fare, and travel as far east as Parliament, south to Front Street, west to Spadina, north to College and Carlton, and return home on a Church Street car, having safely and cheaply circumnavigated the entire main city area.

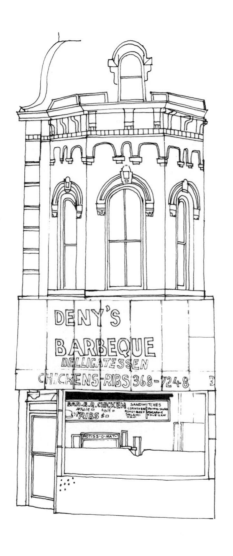

81

Consumers' Gas Offices

The Consumers' Gas Company offices, designed by architect David B. Dick, were built on Toronto Street in 1876. The building is a pleasing amalgam of graceful elegance and businesslike propriety. Its charm derives mainly from the warm buff colour of its stone. This stone was obtained from the Toronto firm of Brown and Love, Builders and Stone Dealers, which was located at the wharf at the foot of Bay Street.

In proportion and ornamental detail the building is classical, employing motifs from a variety of Greek and Roman orders. Egg-and-dart and acanthus leaf mouldings trim the doorway and the entire façade is decorated with classical enrichments in a manner delicate enough not to seem oppressive.

Whether such architectural refinements lightened the burden of paying the gas bill is questionable, but gas consumers were undoubtedly cheered by the steady decrease in rates over the years. From the top price of $5.00 per thousand feet in 1847, the corporation was able to cut back to $3.00 in 1855. By 1906 the price was down to 75¢; five years later another 5¢ was shaved off. Unfortunately, by 1928 the price had crept up to 85¢.

william Roberts. CONSUMER'S GAS CHAMBERS

This handsome structure has weathered its hundred years graciously. Lately it has been deserted by the Consumers' Gas Company and its future is uncertain. Perhaps some prosperous corporation will purchase it, and, as an exercise in conspicuous non-consumption, demonstrate its affluence by refraining from using this prime commercial land for a monolithic office tower.

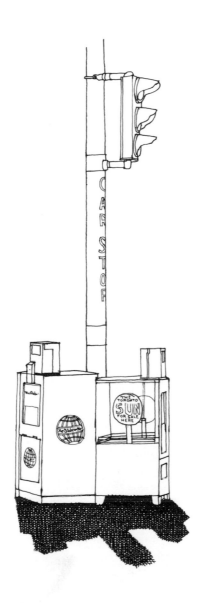

Consumers' Gas Works

This building was a small part of the Consumers' Gas Company's Station "A" which sprawled along Front Street at the south end of Parliament and Berkeley Streets. It was built during the company's expansion of 1887 to 1888 by architects Strickland and Symons. A further expansion was necessary in 1908 and 1912, and Station "B" was erected on Eastern Avenue.

The number of workers engaged in extracting gas from coal had risen from about twenty in 1854 to 690 in 1913. The gas house boys had a reputation for toughness, and rightly so, as the job they did was dirty and dangerous. Perhaps the gas workers patronized the corner saloon at King and Berkeley, stopping in for a 5-cent glass of whiskey or two to wash down the coal dust before they went home. The more aggressive saloon keepers would stand outside their taverns and cajole the homeward-bound workers into dropping in for "just one" — especially on pay day.

At quitting time the workers headed to a home as far away from the gas works as they could afford. As a residential neighbourhood, Gastown was worse than the "other side of the tracks" — the smell of gas hung over all.

Although the building is now occupied by the Toronto Free Theatre, the conversion

William Roberts CONSUMERS GAS.

may have been premature. Currently, the United States Energy Research and Development Administration is investigating a technology known as "coal gasification." It may sound similar to the old process, but it has one important advantage—the coal is not mined but tapped for gas while remaining underground.

Consumers' Gas Company history in Toronto is well documented, since W. H. Pearson, author of *Recollections and Records of Toronto of Old*, worked for the firm from 1854 to 1909. The company was formed in 1847 by Toronto's disgruntled gas users who raised $88,000 the following year to buy the existing works at the foot of Prince's Street from Albert Furniss. Furniss had been providing gas to city subscribers since 1842, but they were dissatisfied both with the poor quality of the gas and the high rates charged ($5.00 per thousand feet), which they termed extortionate.

Henry Thompson was responsible for selling all the shares in the new company, which expanded rapidly. The old Furniss works, "limited in extent and of a very crude nature,"[38] were replaced in 1855 by new buildings at Front and Parliament Streets. Another complete set of works was constructed just over ten years later on lower Berkeley Street.

In the early days of the company, gas consumption was measured in two ways—by meters and by flat rate contract. Customers who chose the latter were placed on the honour system: "Lighting must not commence on any day until the sun has set, and all lights must be extinguished each night within ten minutes after the hour contracted for."[39] (It is not recorded whether inspectors were employed to check up on cheaters.)

The kind of gas sold was manufactured gas derived from coal and intended for illumination. The principle, simplified for children, was explained like this:

> If you fill the bowl of a clay pipe with coal dust, and plug it with clay, and then put the bowl in the fire, the heat will drive out the gas through the tube or stem, when it can be lit as it escapes. On a large scale this is what is done at the gas-works.
>
> Coal is put into iron tubes, called retorts, the gas is driven off by heat, but in an impure state, being mixed with the vapors of ammonia, tar, and sulphur. It has to be put through a process to rid it of impure matters which would dim its light. . . .
>
> Until the gas is wanted, it is stored in the gasholder; this holder is in two parts, the tank and the holder proper. The tank is a pit in the shape of a cylinder which is kept filled with water to prevent leakage of the gas. The holder is above the tank, and is filled with gas. Great care has to be taken to prevent explosions. These do sometimes happen despite caution, shaking the district for miles around and often destroying life.[40]

Another by-product of the gas extraction process was coke, a fuel which produces a quick, hot fire. Coke was used in manufacturing more gas and the surplus sold for fuel. An idea of the size of the Toronto operation is given by their production figures. In 1928, six billion cubic feet of gas was derived using 262,000 tons of coal (in this case from Pennsylvania), 87,000 tons of coke, and 6,400,000 gallons of oil. The by-products obtained were 166,000 tons of coke, 3,875,000 gallons of tar, and 1,205,000 pounds of ammonia.[41]

The primary purpose of gas was the lighting of homes and streets. The street gas lamps had to be turned off and on, morning and night, by lamplighters. In 1884 electric street lights were introduced in Toronto, the first one at the corner of King and Yonge Streets. These were arc lamps, suspended by ropes running through pulleys from iron brackets on wooden poles, and they required regular cleaning and the periodic installation of new carbons.

However, gas fought back. In 1897 the Consumer's Gas Company received permission to sell gas for "heating, cooking, and other than illumination purposes. Its development for these heating purposes, and indeed for every purpose for which controllable heat is required, either in the home or in the industries, has been such, that, although the quantity of gas now used for lighting purposes is negligible, the gas output in a single week in 1928, equals the total quantity sold in 1879."[42]

The Modern Furniture Store

It is not too difficult to discern that the Modern Furniture Store was originally something else. The two Gothic peaks, now blindly shuttered, which rise incongruously above the plate glass overlooking Parliament Street, are decidedly not "modern." They are indicative of a style of architecture, termed "cottage Gothic" which was immensely popular in Ontario soon after the midpoint of the nineteenth century.

In 1850 A. J. Downing, an American writer on architecture, defined a cottage like this:

> What we mean by a cottage, in this country, is a dwelling of small size, intended for the occupation of a family, either wholly managing the household cares itself, or, at the most, with the assistance of one or two servants. The majority of such cottages in this country are occupied, not by tenants, dependents, or serfs, as in many parts of Europe, but by industrious and intelligent mechanics and working men, the bone and sinew of the land, who own the ground upon which they stand, build them for their own use, and arrange them to satisfy their own peculiar wants and gratify their own tastes.[43]

william Roberts   THE MODERN FURNITURE STORE

Despite these stirring sentiments it would seem that the first residents of these cottages were not landlords but merely tenants. During the 1850s the city was pushing north and there was a great amount of land speculation. James Rogers, Hatter, of King Street owned a lot with a fifty-two-foot frontage here in 1857. Four years later a frame cottage owned by Rogers was rented to George Ward, Jeweller, for the sum of $74 per year. In 1871 the two cottages, then owned by George Morse, were evaluated for tax purposes at $900 each. A neighbourly note is struck by the fact that in 1861 Hugh Taylor owned a tavern across the street from these cottages and three years later took over the management of the little "corner store" saloon, the Garibaldi House, down on King at Berkeley Street.

Notes

[1] Robertson, J. R. *Robertson's Landmarks of Toronto*, Volume I.

[2] *Toronto City Directory* advertisement, 1893-94.

[3] *Industries of Canada*.

[4] Middleton, J. E., *National Encyclopedia of Canadian Biography*.

[5] Ibid.

[6] GRIP, *An Independent Journal of Humor and Caricature*, December 26, 1891.

[7] GRIP, November 9, 1878.

[8] Toronto City Archives.

[9] Massey, Vincent. *What's Past Is Prologue*.

[10] Massey, Raymond. *When I Was Young*.

[11] *Industries of Canada*, 1886.

[12] Ibid.

[13] Taylor, C. C. *Toronto "Called Back,"* 1886.

[14] *Industries of Canada*, 1886.

[15] Taylor, C. C. *Toronto "Called Back,"* 1886.

[16] *A Handbook of Toronto*, by A Member of the Press, 1858.

[17] Ibid.

[18] Mulvany, C. Pelham. *Toronto: Past and Present*, 1884.

[19] Grant, Lt. Francis Augustus, aide-de-camp of Governor General Lord Elgin, in a letter to his mother, January 25, 1851. From *St. Lawrence Hall*, Thomas Nelson, publishers.

[20] Downing, A. J. *The Architecture of Country Houses*, 1851.

[21] Scadding, Henry. *Toronto of Old. Collections and Recollections*, 1878.

[22] Jameson, Anna. *Winter Studies and Summer Rambles in Canada*, 1923.

[23] Arthur, Eric. *Toronto, No Mean City*, 1964.

[24] Ruskin, John. *The Seven Lamps of Architecture*, 1890.

[25] 1880's clipping from *Monitor Journal* entered in a temperance scrapbook.

[26] *Mackenzie House*, Toronto Historical Board.

[27] Bowden-Smart, Rodney and Beech, Frank J. *Toronto, An Illustrated Tour Through Its Highways and Byways*, circa 1934.

[28] *Toronto City Directory*.

[29] Mulvany, C. Pelham. *Toronto; Past and Present*, 1884.

[30] Ibid.

[31] Adam, G. Mercer. *Toronto, Old and New: A Memorial Volume*, 1891.

[32] Glazebrook, G. P. de T. *The Story of Toronto*, 1971.

[33] Middleton, J. E. *The Municipality of Toronto*, 1923.

[34] Ryerson, Egerton. *Second Book of Reading Lessons.*

[35] Hodgkins, J. George. *Lovell's General Geography for the Use of Schools*, 1861.

[36] *Industries of Canada*, 1886.

[37] GRIP, 1884.

[38] Pearson, W. H. *Recollections and Records of Toronto of Old*, 1914.

[39] Ibid.

[40] Chase, A. and Clow, E. *Stories of Industry*, 1891.

[41] Bureau of Municipal Research, *Toronto at a Glance*, 1929.

[42] Ibid.

[43] Downing, A. J. *The Architecture of Country Houses*, 1851.

Bibliography

ADAM, G. Mercer. *Toronto, Old and New: A Memorial Volume.*
The Mail Printing Company, Toronto. 1891.

ARTHUR, Eric. *Toronto, No Mean City.*
University of Toronto Press, Toronto, 1964.

ARTHUR, T. S. *Ten Nights In A Bar-Room and What I Saw There.*
J. W. Bradley, Philadelphia, 1860.

BOWDEN-SMART, Rodney and BEECH, Frank J. *Toronto. An Illustrated Tour Through Its Highways and Byways.*
Canadian Gravure Company Limited, Toronto, circa 1934.

BUREAU OF MUNICIPAL RESEARCH. *Toronto at a Glance.*
Toronto, 1929.

CHASE, A. and CLOW, E. *Stories of Industry.* Volume I.
Educational Publishing Company, Boston, New York, Chicago, 1891.

COBB, Lyman. *Cobb's Spelling Book.*
Andrus, Gauntlett and Company, Ithaca, New York. Revised edition, 1835.

DOWNING, A. J. *The Architecture of Country Houses.*
D. Appleton & Company, New York, 1851.

DWIGHT, Nathaniel. *A Short but Comprehensive System of the Geography of the World.* Fourth Northampton Edition, S. & E. Butler, Northampton, 1807.

ELLIS, Norman. *My Parish Is Revolting.*
Paperjacks, General Publishing Company, Don Mills, 1974.

GLAZEBROOK, G. P. de T. *The Story of Toronto.*
University of Toronto Press, 1971.

GRIP, J. W. Bengough, editor. Toronto, 1878-1894.

GUILLET, Edwin C. *Toronto: From Trading Post to Great City.*
Ontario Publishing Company, Limited, Toronto, 1934.

HODGINS, J. George. *Lovell's General Geography for the Use of Schools.*
John Lovell, Montreal and Toronto, 1861.
Industries of Canada. Historical and Commercial Sketches of Toronto and Environs.
M. G. Bixby and Company, Publishers, Toronto, 1886.

JAMESON, Anna. *Winter Studies and Summer Rambles in Canada.*
McClelland and Stewart, Toronto, 1923 and 1965.

MASSEY, Raymond. *When I Was Young.*
McClelland and Stewart, Toronto, 1976.

MASSEY, Vincent. *What's Past Is Prologue:* The Memoirs.
Macmillan, Toronto, 1963.

'A MEMBER OF THE PRESS' A *Handbook of Toronto.*
Lovell and Gibson, Toronto, 1858.

MIDDLETON, Jesse Edgar. *The Municipality of Toronto.*
A History. Three Volumes. Dominion Publishing Company,
Toronto and New York, 1923.

MIDDLETON, Jesse Edgar and DOWNS, W. Scott. *National Encyclopedia of Canadian Biography,* Volume II. Dominion Publishing
Company Ltd., 1937.

MIDDLETON, Jesse Edgar. *Toronto's 100 Years.*
The Centennial Committee, Toronto, 1934.

MULVANY, C. Pelham *Toronto: Past and Present. A Handbook of the
City.*
W. E. Caiger, Publisher, Toronto, 1884.

ONTARIO STATUTES 1916 *Ontario Temperance Act.*

PEARSON, W. H. *Recollections and Records of Toronto of Old.*
Toronto. William Briggs, 1914.

PIPER, John. *Buildings and Prospects.*
The Architectural Press, Westminster, 1948.

READ, David B. *Lives of the Judges of Upper Canada and Ontario from
1791 to the Present.*
Rowsell and Hutchison, Toronto, 1888.

ROBERTSON, John Ross. *Robertson's Landmarks of Toronto.*
Republished from the Evening Telegram, J. R. Robertson,
Toronto, 1894-1908.

RUSKIN, John. *The Seven Lamps of Architecture.*
George Allen, London, 1890.

RYERSON, Egerton. *First Book of Reading Lessons.* Part II.
Canadian Series of School Books. William Warwick & Son,
Toronto, 1880.

RYERSON, Egerton. *Second Book of Reading Lessons.*
Canadian Series of Reading Books. Buntin, Gillies and Company, Hamilton, 1867.

St. Lawrence Hall.
Thomas Nelson and Sons Canada Limited, Toronto and
Montreal, 1969.

SCADDING, Henry. *Toronto of Old.*
Collections and Recollections. Willing and Williamson, Toronto, 1878.

SINCLAIR, Andrew. *Era of Excess, A Social History of the Prohibition
Movement.*
Harper and Row, New York, 1962.

TAYLOR, C. C. *Toronto "Called Back."*
William Briggs, Toronto, 1886.

TORONTO, City Archives Assessment Rolls.
City Directories published mainly by Chewett and Might.

TORONTO HISTORICAL BOARD. *The City of Toronto's Inventory of
Buildings of Architectural and Historical Importance.*
Toronto Historical Board, 1977.

TORONTO HISTORICAL BOARD *Mackenzie House.*

WEBSTER, Noah. *The Elementary Spelling Book.*
D. Appleton and Company, New York. Revised edition, 1866.